SW ANALYSIS

By Christophe Seth

Translation by Carly Probert

Management & Marketing

THE SWOT ANALYSIS

KEY POINTS

- **Name:** The SWOT analysis or SWOT method is an acronym of the terms Strengths, Weaknesses, Opportunities and Threats.
- **Uses:** This model allows organizations (businesses, public administrations or associations) to quickly identify both its internal factors linked to internal functioning and external factors that depend on the environment in which it is evolving. The SWOT analysis is used as a decision-making tool and to facilitate the development of strategic plans.
- **Why is it successful?** The power of the SWOT analysis lies in its simplicity. As well as being simple to use, it also collects results that can be easily communicated to the public.
- **Key Words** :
  - ○ External factor: An element that an organization cannot influence, linked to the environment in which it evolves.
  - ○ Internal factor: An element that can be influenced or modified by the organization.
  - ○ Strengths: Internal factors of the business that reinforce its competitive position.
  - ○ Weaknesses: Internal factors that weaken the competitive position of an organization.
  - ○ Opportunities: External factors that have the power to positively influence the competitive position of an organization.
  - ○ Threats: External factors that negatively influence the external environment of an organization.

INTRODUCTION

History

The SWOT analysis originated from the publication Business Policy: Text and Cases (1965), created by four professors at Harvard University – Edmund Philip Learned (1900-1991), Roland Chris Christensen (1919-1999), Kenneth Richmond Andrews (1916-2005) and William D. Guth. This method is one of the first models to consider the external environment of an organization. Before, strategy models restricted themselves to strategic planning, without taking into account their environment.

Today, the SWOT analysis is mainly used within the marketing departments of large businesses. Many SMBs also use it as a decision-making tool.

A number of consultancy firms also use the SWOT analysis because it allows them to quickly analyze and present their results schematically, and it also simplifies the situation for their clients. Others companies, such as McKinsey and BCG, have their own analysis models.

Definition

The SWOT analysis is a multidimensional tool for strategic analysis:
* It identifies an organization's internal factors (strengths and weaknesses) and its external factors linked to its environment (weaknesses and threats);
* It also allows organizations to prioritize factors in terms of expected impact, whether they are positive (strengths and opportunities) or negative (weaknesses and threats).

A SWOT analysis has no intrinsic value unless it is used for strategic purposes.

THEORY: THE SWOT ANALYSIS

Example of a SWOT analysis

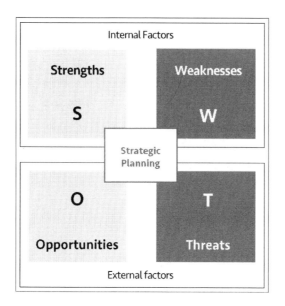

The SWOT analysis investigates the current situation of an organization at a given time, in a forward-looking manner as opposed to a retrospective one. It also analyzes the structure, keeping in mind future perspectives. At the same time, the SWOT analysis focuses on the internal functionality (strengths and weaknesses) and on the external environment (opportunities and threats) of an organization.

- **Strengths** are elements of an organization that positively influence its development and its competitive position. In general, strengths are considered to be particularly significant as they do not characterize the competition. The SWOT analysis identifies the competitive advantages held by a company over its competitors.

- **Weaknesses** are also linked to the internal functioning of an organization, but they generally have a negative impact on its development and its competitive position. The ability to clearly identify the internal weaknesses of an organization is vital : it allows for the improvement of relevant issues and the re-orientation of work in order to make them less vulnerable.
- **Opportunities** for an organization depend on those available in the external environment. They can be exploited to improve progression and competitive position. Once this is done, they can become forces that positively influence the development of an organization.
- **Threats** also originate from the external environment of an organization. Their identification is often the result of traditional strategic work. As long as they are detected in time, threats can be better anticipated and their impact on performance reduced (and vice versa).

Sometimes, threats can become strengths. Likewise, opportunities can become weaknesses. In fact, given that the organization does not develop in its environment alone, its future also depends on the decisions made by competitors.

FACTORS THAT INFLUENCE THE EVOLUTION OF AN ORGANIZATION

In terms of internal functioning, many characteristics are taken into account in order to identify the strengths and weaknesses of an organization, including:

- **Cost competitiveness**. One of the first aspects that make a business competitive is its ability to keep costs low. In order to manage costs, it must closely monitor the efficiency of production technique (Is it possible to produce more using less?) as well as the allocation of resources (Should it substitute capital for labor?). A conflict can arise between cost-competitiveness and worker protection. For example, if lower social and environmental standards can reduce costs, that does not mean that it does not have a (negative) impact on workers;

- **Network and distribution capacity.** Does the company structure have an effective distribution network? In particular, does it guarantee a good delivery service (high rate of products that arrive on time, low rate of breakages, low rate of errors, etc.)? Does it succeed in rationalizing distribution costs (sufficiently low global costs of storage and transport of merchandise). A possible compromise between product quality, delivery time and distribution costs is lower stock levels. This strategy is based on the increasing use of new information technology and communication (NICT). Often referred to as 'just in time production', it means that a company manufactures a product once it is ordered by the customer and is delivered in a very short time due to its effective distribution network;

- **Sales and marketing.** The marketing department also plays a crucial role in the success of a company. Is it in a position to anticipate customer needs? Is it capable of launching publicity campaigns in order to attract customers? A good marketing strategy is an undeniable force for any company;

- **Financial resources.** Sufficient financial stability is a real asset for an organization. In fact, the ability to raise liquidity plays a major role as this is essential for launching any expansion project;

- **Human resources.** The management of human resources is an aspect which is often neglected by companies, public administrations and associations. Nevertheless, it is important that every structure possesses certain key skills among its members. It can be preferable for an organization to spend more time finding a suitable person rather than hurriedly recruiting a candidate that does not match the position. In a more general sense, it is important for companies to establish a system of communication that allows for optimum working relationships between colleagues.

- **Innovation policy.** At a more strategic level, and in our own economy, more and more companies – and universities – are struggling to patent the number of innovations they are capable of. The possession of patents must go hand in hand with strategic vision, allowing the owners to present the usefulness and value of their innovations. They are also influential when negotiating the use of their patented products with other companies.

In terms of the external environment, many factors influence the opportunities and threats faced by an organization, including:

- **Economic climate.** The presence or lack of strong economic growth certainly has an impact on the situation of different organizations. Sound economic activity allows a company to increase its growth. Similarly, a company in difficulty which loses its market shares can sometimes avoid bankruptcy in times of fast economic growth because growth can partially compensate for the weaknesses of a company. We can assume the opposite outcome in cases of economic recession.
- **Global consumer trends.** Another aspect that must not be overlooked by companies is the progression of consumer needs. If the value proposition is consistent with the new needs, the progression is positive. If the needs move away from the value proposition, the progression is negative. In order to avoid this, the marketing department can try to anticipate the changes using different tools such as the life cycle of the product which details the different phases of a product (development, launch, growth, maturity and decline);
- **Competitive environment.** The evolution of the competitive environment also plays a key role. The largest, best performing

companies or those more likely to start a price war can have a negative impact on the profitability of a company;

- **Regulatory environment.** The evolution of regulations can also create a threat if a structure is not prepared to face them. However, in certain cases it allows companies to avoid their competitors if they are less prepared to compete.

Now that you understand the theoretical foundation of the SWOT analysis, you can have some fun and create your own analysis as a student or worker. For example, if you are in the middle of your studies, you may have excellent general knowledge (strength), but you sometimes have trouble expressing your ideas in writing (weakness). As a student, you have access to a considerable number of opportunities (Erasmus, work placements, etc.). However, the changes in the cost of living can unfortunately cause problems for you (threat).

LIMITS AND EXTENSIONS OF THE MODEL

CRITICISMS

Theorists and practitioners generally agree that the results of a SWOT analysis can lead to a quick analysis of the situation, which remains approximate and incomplete. Also, the different aspects of the SWOT analysis do not necessarily exclude each other.

For example, a new regulation can be perceived as both a threat and an opportunity for a business. Consultants Terry Hill and Roy Westbrook published a seminal paper SWOT Analysis: It's Time for a Product Recall which brings to light the inherent limits of a SWOT analysis.

- Firstly, it remains essentially descriptive. It has been shown in certain cases that this makes it ineffective as it does not guide the decision-making process in one way or another. The diagnostic of a SWOT analysis could be excellent, but if decisions made in advance are not correct or are not correctly implemented, it is useless. We can therefore see that the SWOT analysis is not really a means of competitive advantage.
- We cannot overlook the costs involved in the establishment of a SWOT analysis because it requires a fee for the internal and/or external consultants. It is sometimes preferable not to be restricted by a managerial model that limits creativity.
- Another risk comes from not prioritizing the identified factors according to the SWOT analysis in order of importance and focusing on insignificant details. Besides wasting time, this could have a disastrous impact on an organization if it spends on resources to eliminate minor problems.

OTHER MODELS

There are other models that seem as effective as the SWOT analysis and facilitate decision-making just as well. The five forces analysis by Michael E. Porter (American university lecturer, born in 1947) evaluates, for example, the constraints to which an industry is subject. Others focus on strategic interaction between competitors (e.g. decisions linked to production quantity and the fixation of prices). They supply a less comprehensive approach, but are still powerful tools for evaluating the power of the competition within the analyzed industries.

Porter's five forces

Porter's five forces model enables a company to analyze its competitive environment. It identifies five forces that are able to influence an industry's competitive landscape.

- The most evident constraint faced by a company is the **existence of direct competitors**. However, the intensity of the rivalry between companies does not depend systematically on a number of companies being in competition: It is possible that two companies within industry A could be in a price battle whilst four companies within industry B form a stable and profitable cartel.
- The **threat of new entrants** can also discourage a company from fixing high prices, even in monopolist cases. This threat is not always believable if there are significant barriers at the entrance and exit of the industry, in which case the return is negligible. Certain companies invest in an excess capacity in order to produce more if a competitor arrives (which effectively reduces prices and lowers the profit of new entrants) The new entrants, being generally up to date with these excess capacities, are less inclined to launch.

- Companies must be aware of **products and services that could replace them**. If we look at the example of medium and long-haul transport (between 300 and 1,000 km), high-speed trains have become a serious substitute for air travel in Western Europe over the past few decades (which has led to a rationalization of the air sector with the emergence of low cost operators such as Ryanair and easy Jet).

- **The power of negotiation between suppliers and customers** can have a decisive impact on the profitability of a company. Generally, you could say that customers and suppliers can obtain better prices when there are only a few companies and potential new entrants are appearing on the market.

Representation of Porter's five forces model

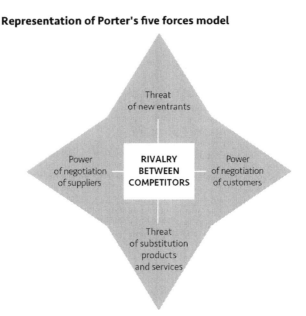

Oligopolistic competition and the presence of cartels

Some economic models let us focus on the strategic interaction between companies.

- **Antoine Augustin Courmot's model** (French mathematician and philosopher, 1801-1877) was created to analyze the oligopolistic competition (belonging to a market characterized by a small number of sellers for a large number of buyers). It is generally used until the companies decide what quantities to produce – a decision made in terms of the influence on pricing policy. Active companies in the automobile industry, for example, find it difficult to raise their short-term production capacity (constructing a factory takes time). For a number of competitors, the pressure of competition in a Cournot-style industry is generally considered to be average and limited.

- On the contrary, **Joseph Louis François Bertrand's model** (French mathematician and economist, 1822-1900) is used until companies decide their pricing levels and can increase or decrease the quantity produced with ease. As long as there is competition as Bertrand describes, two companies are enough to keep profits low, because they will inevitably find themselves in a price battle. This model is mainly used by companies in industries where it is easy to modify the short-term quantity of production concerned with such competition (e.g. the textile industry). In general, if there are at least two competitors, the pressure of competition in a Bertrand-style industry is very strong. Such industries are, therefore, less attractive to begin with.

- • It is also possible for active competitors within an industry – although this is illegal – to explicitly agree to limit competition. This is known as an **organized cartel**. Informal agreements are not illegal and are, by definition, impossible to prove. If a cartel is stable, the joint profit of the companies concerned will be equal to the monopolist profit. In summary, the following conditions facilitate the forming of a cartel:

- A low number of companies;
- The capacity to quickly detect and punish those who don't respect the agreement;
- Sufficient patience of the companies participating in the agreement.

APPLICATIONS

FIVE STEPS FOR SUCCESS WITH THE SWOT ANALYSIS

1. **Identify strengths**. Identify the elements that have a positive influence on the performance of the organization and are linked to the internal functioning. As mentioned in the chapter presenting the model, it is useful to thoroughly carry out this identification by combining what characterizes the financial situation of the organization, the performance of its distribution channel, its brand image, etc.

2. **Identify weaknesses**. Next, identify the elements that have a negative influence on the performance of an organization and those linked to the internal functioning. A weak capacity for innovation, bad communication and an incapability to reduce costs like other competitors are all weaknesses that negatively affect the performance of an organization.

3. **Identify opportunities**. When considering the opportunities offered by a defined environment, they are external factors of an organization that could have a positive influence. The aspects to investigate are more or less specific to each organization (competition, economic context, legal and demographic, etc.).

4. **Identify threats**. When identifying threats in a defined environment, it is useful to analyze the external factors of an organization that could have a negative influence. Once again, the elements requiring investigation depend on the nature of each organization.

5. **Establish a strategy**. Once all of the internal and external factors are identified, the decision-making phase can begin. Sometimes this can take the form of long-term strategic planning. In other

cases, the SWOT analysis will only speed up of decision-making by taking into account the context in which the organization evolves.

ADVICE

- It is essential to support your findings with figures, data and facts. A diagnosis made too quickly is the perfect way to make bad decisions.
- If possible, try to also back up each strength, weakness, opportunity and threat. This eliminates negligible factors that don't have useful influence over decision-making.
- The SWOT analysis is valuable only if exploited. It is essential to ensure that the decisions made are well implemented.
- When deciding to make decisions based on the results of a SWOT analysis, concentrate all efforts on the decisions that the organization is able to put in place or control.

CASE STUDY – TOURISM ORGANIZATION IN THE SOUTH OF FRANCE

In this section we will look at an example of a SWOT analysis. The organization studied is a small tourism organization managed by a couple. They own three guest houses located in the south of France, on the border of the Alps and Provence. Identified as a tourism organization, they attract a customer base that is mainly foreign, particularly in summer. One of the major problems affecting this tourism organization is the irregularity in demand according to the season. The occupancy rate is close to 100% in July and August, yet it barely reaches 30% during the rest of the year. The occupancy problem is directly linked to the external environment of the company, since it goes without saying that the couple running the guest houses doesn't have any control over the holiday dates of customers. However, there are other factors that can be adjusted and thus controlled internally in order to influence the choices of tourists.

Let's look at how a SWOT analysis can help to enhance this tourism organization.

Analysis of the external environment of the company – Threats and opportunities

- **The evolution of regulations** has had a considerable impact on the situation of this small organization over the last few years. They represent a real constraint, in the sense that the owners must sometimes spend large amounts of money to satisfy them. We can, for example, think about new security regulations, which sometimes apply in a similar way to large hotels, as they benefit from important economies of scale (the average cost per room in order to satisfy regulations decreases as the number of rooms increases) and generally possess more modern buildings.

- **The evolution of fiscal policy** in a foreign country can often have a crucial impact on the operations of a company, in an indirect manner. In the case of this tourism organization, which attracts a number of Belgian clients with more affluent social-professional profiles, it is possible that the adjustment to Belgian taxation on company cars has consequently caused a reduction of occupancy rates. In fact, it would seem that the fiscal reform in question has made aid for company cars less interesting to Belgian companies, which mostly provide free petrol for staff benefiting from such a vehicle. The use of a car to travel to the South of France is particularly useful for Belgians, particularly those with young children. Also, in the event that this system is used less, customers tend to change their habits and, at the same time, think about other modes of transport and other destinations that are farther away and less exotic. This last point leads to the problem of substitution products and services developed in Porter's five forces model (e.g. Journeys by airplane for which the relative price represents significant competition).

- **The evolution of technology** is both an opportunity and a threat for the young couple. The introduction of websites that allow users to book a room directly – without going through the owners – has considerably changed the management of guest houses. This technological revolution creates an opportunity in the sense that these sites increase visibility and can facilitate contact between owners and tourists. Unfortunately, it is often difficult to control your online reputation when using these services. The increasingly frequent habit of tourists using these websites to book rooms has caused a near disappearance of paper guides, in which the tourism infrastructure is often well referenced.
- **The role of public powers in the promotion of tourism in the region.** Public powers have a considerable influence over the appeal of a region. In the case of this tourism establishment, the support and promotion of surrounding places and/or activities (e.g. places of natural beauty, one-off sporting events, etc.) by the local government, for example, can attract more customers.
- **The accessibility by air, rail and road.** Given the difficulty involved in accessing the tourism establishment, it is recommended that managers support the developments of investment proposals in transport infrastructure (e.g. highways, railway lines, airport terminals, etc.).
- **The disadvantaged economic environment** linked to the crisis has obviously had a direct negative impact on the desires of tourists to go on holiday: the estimated expenditure budget actually seems less important than in 2008. On the other hand, the much awaited return of economic growth could have a positive impact on the situation of this tourism establishment.

Analysis of the internal environment of the organization – Strengths and weaknesses

- **Tourist satisfaction.** The level of tourist satisfaction is good. Not only is this a sign of a successful organization, but it is also important as it attracts new customers by word of mouth and the online reputation created as a result (a good online brand image). Many tourists can become loyal customers and come back every year. Some even become true ambassadors of the establishment and encourage their friends and family to go there on holiday.

- **The location of the tourism establishment** is both attractive and off-putting. The geographical isolation of the place attracts a certain type of tourist who wants a break in a calm environment, in which case this establishment is perfect. This location can also be seen as a weakness in the sense that the guest houses are difficult to access by public transport and they are far away from amenities (supermarkets, restaurants, etc.). Also, the region is not very well known by tourists.

- **The proximity to activities and tourism services.** The availability of diverse sporting activities, including seasonal activities (hiking trails and mountain biking in the summer ; skiing in the winter) nearby the accommodation is a definite strength for the organization. Equally, the hosting of set meals can also put tourists in contact with each other. Many of them appreciate this social contact, even if some do prefer their privacy.

- **Customer profile.** Currently, the organization attracts mainly private individuals. It could be interesting to attract a different client base. Contacting companies looking to organize seminars and/or team building sessions is a possible solution. Another possibility is collaborating with providers of tourism services, such as hiking organizations.

- **Internet connection quality.** The internet connection is slow due to the isolated location which is a considerable weakness in this digital era.

SWOT analysis of the guest house example

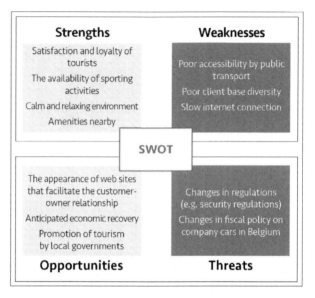

The SWOT analysis has enabled us to identify a certain number of strengths, weaknesses, opportunities and threats of the organization. Now let's observe how the combination of these elements can lead to making efficient strategic decisions. From this point on, it is possible to:

- **Take advantage of opportunities.** The evolution of technology can be utilized with regards to the visibility offered by the internet. The organization would be wise to register its guest houses on the available platforms where prospective customers (people looking for a remote holiday location) can find them. Given that consumers have a lower holiday budget than before, it could be useful for the organization to adapt its pricing policy, taking particular advantage of the possibilities offered by new technology (e.g. last minute offers).;

- **Anticipate threats.** Even if the evolution of the regulatory framework can be considered a short term threat, it is also an obstacle to the development of new structures. In the long run, they will form an excellent barrier at the entrance and allow those who adapt to the new regulatory framework to benefit from stability in the face of competition;
- **Reinforce strengths.** Word of mouth could be the most effective method if the organization communicates better with its regular clients in order to attract them during other seasons. Their loyalty can also be harnessed through social networks;
- **Fix some weaknesses.** To diversify the client base, the business could propose stays to corporate clients (organizing a professional seminar stay or a themed stay involving gastronomy, sports or any equivalent).

Other decisions could also be made and other opinions could undoubtedly be considered, but in the end, everything will depend on the priorities established by those responsible for the organization.

SUMMARY

- The SWOT analysis involves the analysis of factors that influence (positively or negatively) the internal functioning and the external environment of an organization, which could be a business, an association or a public administration.
- The strengths and weaknesses are the measures that an organization can control. Cost-competitiveness evidently plays a determining role in the success of a business. One should never underestimate the role played by the competition concerning other things, notably the capacity for innovation.
- Opportunities and threats are linked to the external environment of an organization and cannot be controlled by them. They are often thought to be economic (growth or recession), but it is important not to ignore other aspects that are more specific to the industry (changing customer needs, competitive environment and regulations).
- The study of strengths, weaknesses, opportunities and threats should lead to decision-making or the adoption of strategy plans.
- Some advice for carrying out a SWOT analysis: Think about basing it on facts rather than institutions. It is crucial to back up your analysis with tangible figures (e.g. financial data).
- The SWOT analysis is currently a very popular method, particularly within marketing departments of large companies.
- Its simplicity remains a double-edged sword. Some authors have shown that the use of the SWOT analysis can sometimes have a negative impact on an organization's performance. Negative effects can be a lack of rigor or the analysis not being followed by the recommended strategic action plan (according to Terry Hill and Roy Westbrook).

- Other models have been developed to facilitate the establishment of strategic planning:
  ○ The five forces model, created by Michael E. Porter at the end of the seventies, focuses mainly on the constraints that negatively influence the profitability of a business;
  ○ Other alternatives to the SWOT analysis developed in the 19th century, the models of French economists Antoine Augustin Cournot and Joseph Bertrand, enable the thorough analysis of competition in the required context.

FURTHER READING

- 'L'art de (bien) utiliser une matrice SWOT pour convaincre', in *I LIKE PM*, accessed 6th June 2014. http://www.ilikepm.com/2010/08/02/lart-de-bien-utiliser-une-matrice-swot-pour-convaincre/
- 'Préparer une analyse SWOT', in *BCV*, accessed 6th June 2014. http://www.bcv.ch/fr/entreprises/outils_et_conseils/creer_votre_entreprise/d_une_idee_a_un_plan/votre_produit_ou_service_a_t_il_un_potentiel_de_vente_sur_le_marche/preparer_une_analyse_swot
- Bouvier-Patron (Paul), *Entreprise et innovation. Vers l'inter-organisation innovante responsable ?*, Paris, L'Harmattan, 2011.
- 'Fiche technique. L'analyse SWOT', in *Université du Québec à Montréal*, accessed 6th June 2014. http://www.er.uqam.ca/nobel/r20014/Referentiel/21_Reflexion_Strategique/SWOT.pdf
- Helms (Marilyn M.), 'Encyclopedia of Management Theory. SWOT Analysis Framework', in *Sage Knowledge*, 2013, accessed 6th June 2014. http://www.sagepub.com/gray3e/study/chapter3/Encyclopaedia%20entries/SWOT_Analysis_Framework.pdf
- Hill (Terry) & Westbrook (Roy), 'SWOT Analysis: It's Time for a Product Recall', in *Long Range Planning*, vol. 30, n° 1, February 1997, p. 46-52.
- Lambin (Jean-Jacques) & Moerloose (Chantal de), *Marketing stratégique et opérationnel. Du marketing à l'orientation-marché*, 7th edition, Paris, Dunod, 2008.
- 'L'analyse SWOT', in *European Commission*, accessed 6th June 2014. http://ec.europa.eu/europeaid/evaluation/methodology/examples/too_swo_res_fr.pdf
- Learned (Edmund Philip), Christensen (Roland), Andrews (Kenneth) & Guth (William), *Business Policy – Text and Cases*, 1st édition, Homewood, Irwin, 1965.

- Mayrhofer (Ulrike), *Management stratégique*, 1st édition, Paris, Bréal, 2007.
- Porter (Michael E.), 'The Five Competitive Forces That Shape Strategy', in *Harvard Business Review*, January 2008, p. 23-41.
- Rousseau (Benoist), 'Analyses SWOT', in *ANDLIL*, accessed 6th June 2014. http://www.andlil.com/analyses-swot/
- Van Laethem (Nathalie), 'L'analyse SWOT : 10 conseils pour la réussir', in *Le blog de la stratégie marketing*, accessed 6th June 2014. http://www.marketing-strategie. fr/2010/05/15/10-conseils-pour-reussir-lanalyse-s-w-o-t/
- Varian (Hal), *Introduction à la microéconomie*, 7th edition, Brussels, De Boeck, 2011

www.50minutes.com

Publisher: Lemaitre Publishing
Rue Lemaitre 6 | BE-5000 Namur
info@lemaitre-editions.com

ISBN ebook: 978-2-8062-6583-8
Paper ISBN: 978-2-8062-6932-4
Cover photo: © Lisiane Detaille

Digital conception: Primento,
the digital partner of publishers.

Printed in Great Britain
by Amazon